FOLK HARP

MEL BAY PRESENTS

Great French Composers for Folk Harp

by Sunita Staneslow

1 2 3 4 5 6 7 8 9 0

Visit us on the Web at www.melbay.com — E-mail us at email@melbay.com

Table of Contents

About the Author

Sunita Staneslow has been playing music since she was a child, and has been a professional performer, teacher and arranger since 1985. She studied with teachers in her native Minnesota and has traveled to learn from some of the great harpists of our time in New York, Paris, and Tel Aviv. She graduated from Tufts University in Medford, Massachusetts and earned a Masters Degree from Manhattan School of Music.

After completing graduate school, Sunita's Scottish husband bought her a clarsach (Scottish folk harp). Together they traveled around the world for one year, harp in tow. Inspired by this experience, Sunita began performing folk music from a variety of traditions. She enjoys performing both on her larger pedal harp and her Scottish clarsach and uses both instruments for the different styles of music that she performs. Sunita's passion is arranging music for the lever harp and her work has been recognized by the American Harp Society, The Scottish Clarsach (harp) Society and the International Society for Folk Harpers and Craftsmen. She has released over 15 recordings in addition to appearing as a guest on numerous other CDs. Sunita moved to Israel in the summer of 2000 and continues to tour North America and Europe several times a year teaching and performing at festivals and concerts.

www.sunitaharp.com

Fais do-do

Go to Sleep

Traditional French
Arr. by Sunita Staneslow

La fille de Parthenay

The Girl from Parthenay

Traditional 19th Century France
Arr. by Sunita Staneslow

8

Medieval Melody

Richard de Fournival
Arr. by Sunita Staneslow

11

Derriere Chez Nous

Near Our Old Home

Traditional French
Arr. by Sunita Staneslow

Tenès la de Près

Hold Tight to Your Girl

Traditional Rigaudon from Cevennes
Arr. by Sunita Staneslow

14

La laine de nos moutons

The Wool of Our Sheep

Traditional Song from Auvergne
Arr. by Sunita Staneslow

Menuet

Jean Philippe Rameau (1683-1764)
Arr. by Sunita Staneslow

Set F♯ IV

Moderato

Menuet

Henry Purcell (1659-1695)
Arr. by Sunita Staneslow

La fille aux cheveux de lin

The Girl with the Flaxen Hair (excerpt)

Claude Debussy (1832-1918)
Arr. by Sunita Staneslow

Calm and sweet

 = Muffle

Rêverie

(excerpt)

Claude Debussy (1862-1918)
Arr. by Sunita Staneslow

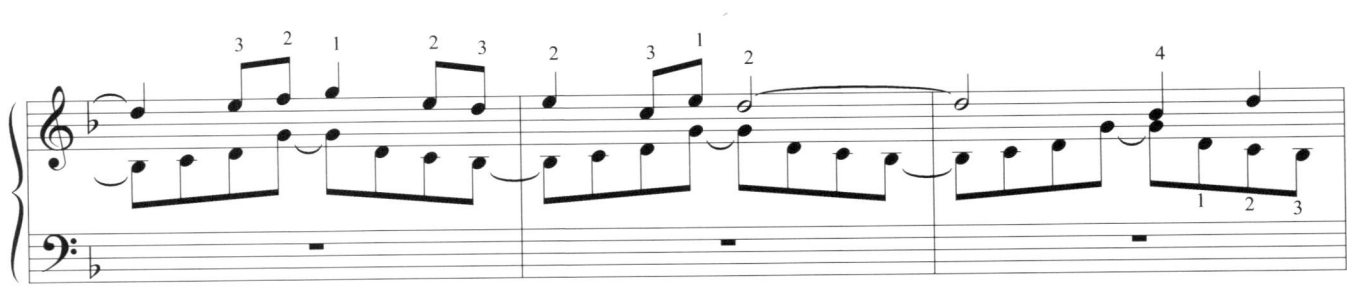

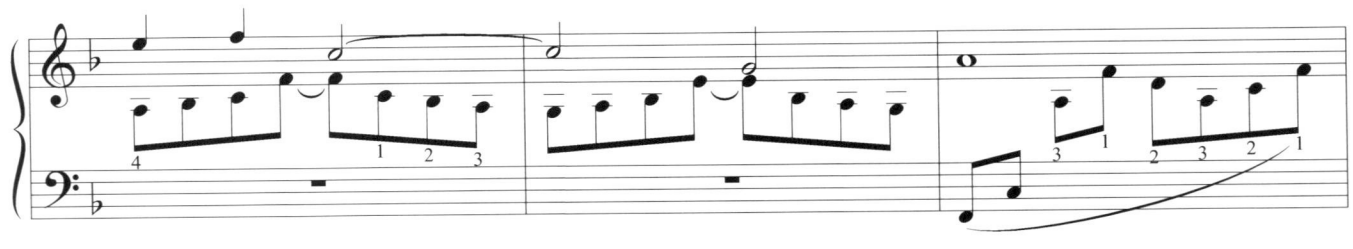

Clair de lune

(Excerpt)

Claude Debussy (1862-1918)
Arr. by Sunita Staneslow

Romance
(Excerpt)

Claude Debussy (1862-1918)
Arr. by Sunita Staneslow

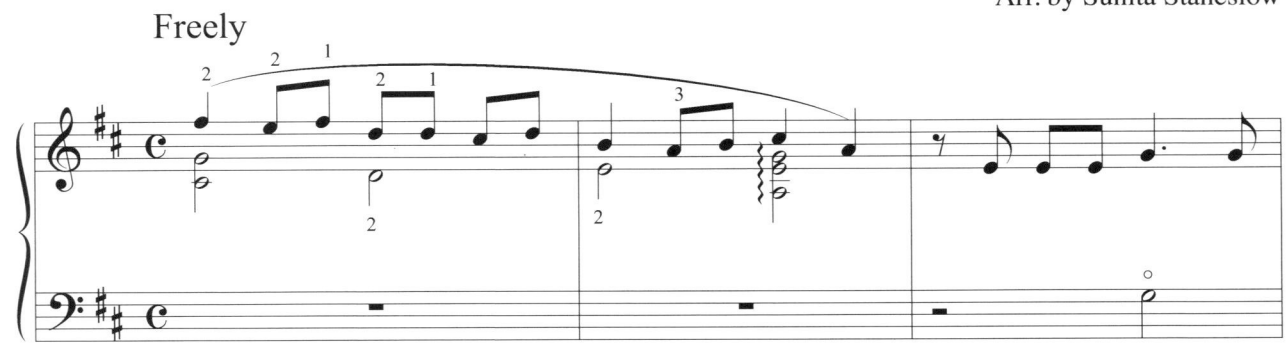

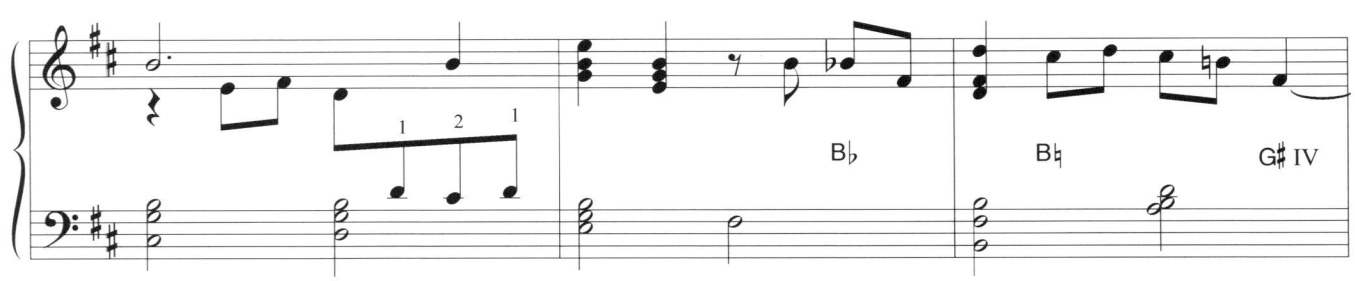

Pavane

(Excerpt)

Maurice Ravel (1875-1937)
Arr. by Sunita Staneslow

Première Gymnopédie

Erik Satie (1866-1925)
Arr. by Sunita Staneslow

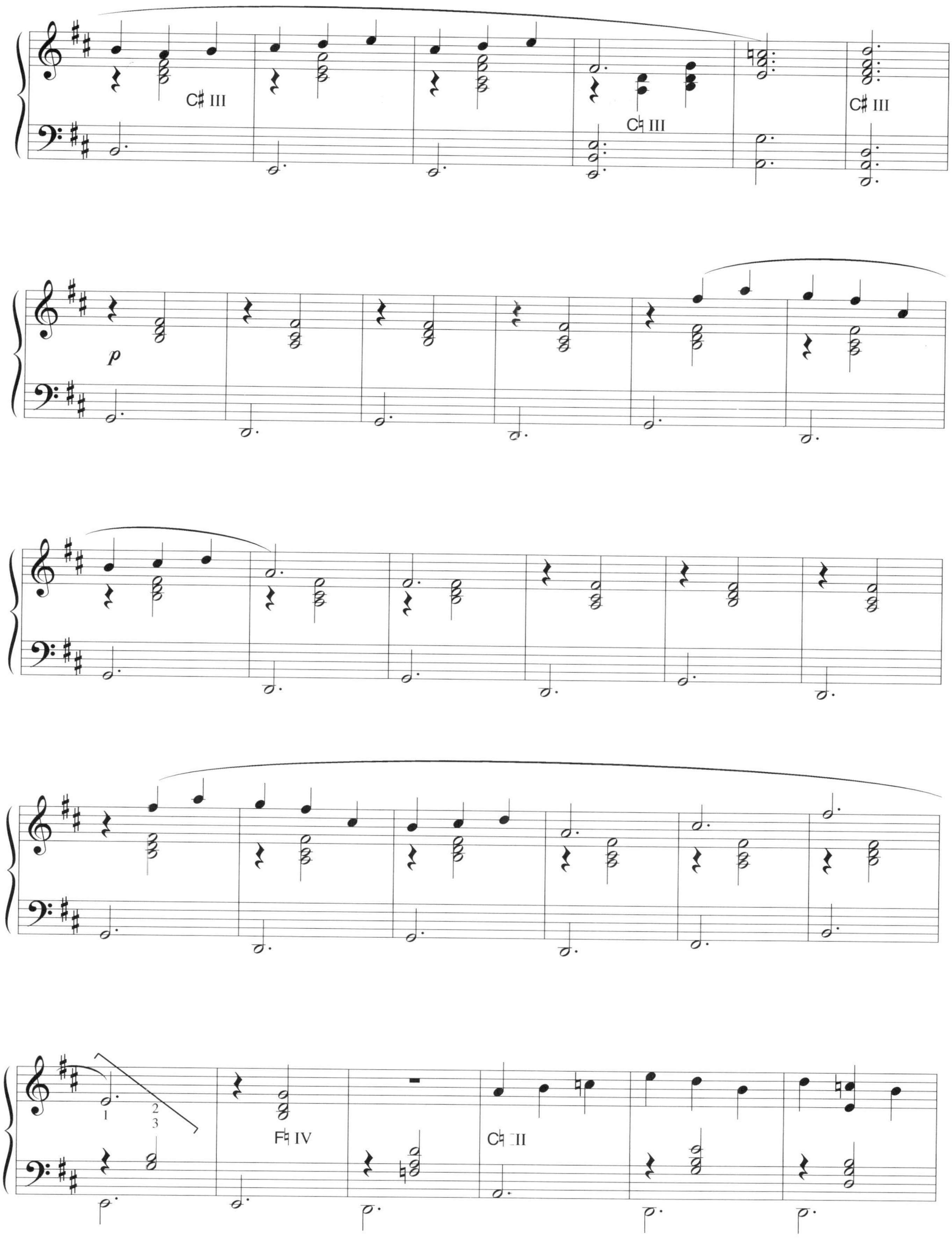
C♯ III
C♮ III
C♯ III
p
1
2
3
F♮ IV
C♮ II

Made in the USA
Monee, IL
11 June 2026

52191937R00020